THE CEO'S GUIDE TO TALENT ACQUISITION

GINNI GARNER
TIM TOLAN
RUSS RIENDEAU, PH.D.

eyecatcher

An Eyecatcher Press Nonfiction Book

Library of Congress Cataloging-in-Publication Data
ISBN   978-0-9654631-3-3
Riendeau, Russ, Tolan, Tim, Garner, Ginni
        The CEO's Guide to Talent Acquisition
        "An Eyecatcher Press nonfiction book."
        ISBN (alk. paper)
        1. Employees—Recruiting. 2. Management.
        3. Sales personnel.
I. Title.

Cover design by The Pepper Group
Printed in the United States of America
Printing by Press Tech

Table of Contents

Foreword

I felt a strong tap on my shoulder as I made my way through the crowded lobby, shaking hands and being introduced to dozens of business leaders.

"Hello, Dr. Cohn, we wanted to thank you for that great presentation. Your message about the importance of innovation was very inspiring, and it was exciting to see the work being done on the forefront of medicine. In fact, two co-authors and I are in the final stages of writing a book for CEOs on talent acquisition and retention, and we were wondering if you would consider writing the foreword. I'm going to call you in two days, and I will say the words 'purple elephant' to jog your memory. I'll tell you more about the book then, and we'll see if you're interested. Thanks again."

This brief dialogue took place in a crowded auditorium in Atlanta where I had just finished a 45-minute address to about 1000 CEOs and key executives who were attending the regional meeting of Vistage International, the largest CEO organization in the world. In the address, I described some of the cutting-edge technology that is being developed at the Texas Heart Institute at St. Luke's Episcopal Hospital in Houston and shared my vision of what treatments might be available for patients suffering from cardiovascular disease in the not-too-distant future.

Ginni, Tim, and Russ called me two days later with the codename "purple elephant," and I immediately recalled our introduction. They shared the book's concept and what value they intended to provide CEOs as it related to talent acquisition and retention. It was a little out of my area of expertise, but it sounded interesting, so I agreed to read the manuscript.

As I read and reflected on what the book was about, I considered the mixed similarities in the medical field and the business world. As a cardiac surgeon and surgical innovator, my goal is to continue to evolve the tools and techniques that we use every day in heart surgery to make what we do less invasive, safer, and more reproducible. To do that, we critically evaluate the advantages and disadvantages of each step in a procedure and try to identify those that cause more risk than benefit to the patient. We then try to redesign the procedure, often through the integration of new technology, to eliminate or mitigate the risky parts. Frequently this requires us to look with an open mind at technology used in a different specialty, or even fields outside the realm of medicine.

It now seems clear to me that CEOs have to do the

same type of analysis to stay competitive in our rapidly changing world and to advocate for the health of the corporation. Specifically, they must perform the same sort of analysis in the identification, attraction, and retention of talented workers. Like a surgeon scrutinizing the steps in a procedure, an effective CEO must dissect the different elements involved in a task and figure out what are the really important skills and traits that are vital in key employees. Moreover, he or she must be able to identify the presence or absence of these traits in prospective employees. Like medical innovators, CEOs must be innovative in their efforts to "out-hire" the competition, and must resort to creative solutions to find, attract, and retain what they are looking for, frequently utilizing elements from outside fields.

Interestingly, I think the primary objectives of CEOs and physicians are rather similar as well. As doctors, we feel a great sense of responsibility in looking after the wellness of our patients. Due to the incredible complexity of human physiology, total patient care frequently involves numerous specialists working in close collaboration to salvage a critical patient. We rely on expert nursing care in the operating room and postoperatively in the intensive care unit, as well as skilled anesthesiologists and perfusionists to keep the patient alive and stable while we are working inside the heart. After surgery, it is not unusual, for example, for a heart surgeon to consult a pulmonologist (lung doctor), electrophysiologist (heart rhythm doctor), hematologist (specialist in disorders of blood clotting), infectious disease specialist, and gastroenterologist (stomach and intestine doctor) to help manage a challenging case. The surgeon must ensure that each physician he consults has the requisite skills and is like-minded in his or her approach to the practice of medicine and expectations in patient outcome. Without ensuring the right personnel, and, more importantly, the right collection of skills, it is impossible to ensure the health of the patient. In a very similar way, the CEO must advocate for the wellness of the corporation. This requires accurate diagnosis of issues that need addressing, and identification of individuals who have the required skills to address them. Moreover, the corporation must be monitored closely, like a critical patient, to ensure the "treatment" is proceeding as planned.

As you read this dynamic and engaging book, I encourage you to keep asking the question, "What is it about my company and my co-workers that makes us unique, and how can I focus my efforts through expanding my skilled workforce to capitalize on our strengths?" With this idea in mind, I believe you'll identify many strategies within these pages, some that take only minutes to implement, that will have an immediate favorable effect, and that will guide you to become better at getting to the heart of your employees' true skills and passions. Who knows? Maybe you'll also be helping to reduce healthcare costs for your employees by creating a more vibrant, less stressful, and healthier workplace.

I wish you much success in your life and business,

William Cohn, M.D.
Director, Minimally Invasive Surgical Technology
Texas Heart Institute
December 1, 2007

Preface

So critical is this topic of talent acquisition and retention in business that the September 15/16, 2007, weekend edition of *The Wall Street Journal* dedicated a section—the lead story titled "How to Fill the Talent Gap"—to uncovering the essential issues surrounding this topic of talent acquisition.

Interestingly, the entire article, written in collaboration with *MIT Sloan Management Review*, never once addressed the most important key and critical step when it comes down to the talent acquisition issue: You first must learn how to identify the right person for the job. Period. Any additional training, motivational tool, or leadership coaching introduced after the person is employed will be most effective only for the persons who fit the profile and culture deeply engrained in the company. Luck is not a strategy.

Essential elements that any successful organization's talent acquisition/human resource charter that is under the watchful eye of a CEO must contain:

1. Clearly defined job descriptions customized for the positions, which include key initiatives and goals for the next 12 months. These goals must be measurable and realistic.

2. A list of skill sets required to perform effectively. Skill sets and competencies can be transferred to nearly any industry, providing the company has an adequate training program.

3. A simple, validated, and benchmarked psychometric tool that allows hiring managers to review results from face-to-face interviews, samples of the candidate's written work, as well as the psychology-related issues of personality style, temperament, leadership philosophy, and competencies in critical thinking. Combining all these components will give a stronger representation of the candidate's abilities. Thus, better hires.

4. New Hire Survey showing various industries that other employees came from prior to joining the company. This list will make future recruiting easier and tactical.

5. Behavioral-based interviewing training or similar training that is delivered to every hiring manager in the company at least once a year. This training must provide critical thinking and questioning methodologies that allow hiring managers a broader base of assessment tools to discover talent your competitors have overlooked.

6. A defined and written-down key competitive advantage of why a person should work for your

organization. This competitive advantage must be distinct to attract the top talent in business today.

Oddly enough, these six simple standards were not mentioned in the *Journal* article on talent acquisition. In our opinion, these six standards are critical and create the first defense against hiring the wrong person for the job or hiring a person based solely on gut intuition, waiting for the purple squirrel (the "perfect candidate") to appear, which can result in hiring the wrong person. Behavioral interviews, assessments, 180-degree references, and even requesting a written strategic plan for the candidate's first 30–120 days are essential ingredients leading up to any smart hiring decision.

Such tools and metrics, used on a regular basis, provide a strong insurance policy against wrong hires, and ensure more effective results from your motivational efforts and additional training.

If you read no further in this book, please paste this list of six hiring standards into your PDA and send a copy to your human resources department immediately to build a strategy around all six. You will see a dramatic difference in the level of talent you're able to choose from, attract to your company, as well as retain. Get the right talent on board and they're going to be happier and more productive leaders. So will you.

—Ginni, Tim, and Russ

Introduction

Consider for a moment the issues affecting you as a leader in business today:

- Human capital shortages due to demographic shifts in an aging workforce
- Generational/cultural differences in workplace attitudes and project-oriented work
- Global pressure toward "greening" of the planet
- Pajama management: managing a remote and mobile workforce
- Record low unemployment levels
- Media and instant news coverage
- Internet access to more than 80 percent of American households
- Increased competition from foreign markets and online purchasing
- Healthcare costs increasing
- Diversity hiring challenges
- An increasingly litigious society
- War and terrorism
- A bright and dynamic workforce in search of great places to work

Wow! You, the 21st-century leader, have some exciting challenges in attracting and retaining top executives who will be expected to lead and grow your organization amid an ever-changing business landscape. Still, even with all the issues mentioned, the primary issue that drives and sustains successful businesses is the acquisition and retention of human capital. Get the right people on your team and all the other issues become manageable, fixable, changeable—and profitable.

Fact: The number-one issue facing CEOs and leaders today is identifying, attracting, and retaining top talent. This book provides fast, proven, immediate, easy-to-implement ideas to help you attract and retain top talent right now. Every newspaper, every business magazine, every corporate HR executive is examining and exploring better ways to secure and retain talented workers. To secure and retain talent, you as a leader must utilize an aggregate of "intelligences." You must be able to cultivate human capital, hold and execute a vision for the future of the company, and possess a leadership style that delivers to the bottom line fast. The only way to spread the workload, identify new opportunities, and create solutions is to secure great people.

As a business leader in today's exciting and lightning-speed marketplace, you could be managing a team spread out across the globe, working from balconies atop boulders in Colorado, glaciers in Iceland, houseboats in the Puget Sound, a cabin on Mt. Hood, or a sleek Tartan 10 moored in brilliant blue water off St. Thomas. These employees are speaking dozens of languages, interfacing with cutting-edge technology, and possessing skill sets you may not be able to define, let alone appreciate. Conversely, you could be a small consulting company or midsized services provider in search of ways to expand your business. How can you better manage such a diverse and shifting workforce? We have the answer. This book contains three elements busy readers—and publishers— demand from a successful business book:

1. A fast read—people are too busy. This book clocks in at 42 minutes flat from cover to cover.
2. Immediate and easy-to-implement ideas. Finish the book—change something/fix something right now.
3. Humor. Life is serious enough.

We believe this book hits all the marks. It is a collection of our experiences in the world of executive search, management consulting, and leadership roles, hyperfocused with real-world stories that drive key points you can use to attract and retain the best talent. From understanding legal challenges to determining a "fast fit" to understanding compensation for performance and retention, to writing an effective job spec, this book will provide you and your key executives the metrics and framework to secure great talent.

Section I

Attracting Top Talent:
The Coolest Magnet Wins

People come and go so quickly here…
—Dorothy, The Wizard of Oz

Sell the thunder.
They'll buy the rain.

*Does your company offer "potential"
to a prospective employee?*

We recently reviewed the past 100 placements our search firms made and found. Amazingly enough, more than 40 percent of these positions did not exist 36 months ago! Are you willing to sell the opportunity to potential hires that they can define and create a new job for themselves? Is there a worn trail to prove it? Will you design a new incentive plan to reward dynamic sales growth or innovative product marketing ideas? Does your culture promote this entrepreneurial spirit?

Sell the thunder, sell the opportunity. It's loud, demands attention, and has energy. But after you've sold the thunder, offer a steady, nurturing rain of support, freedom, and reward. You will attract the elite to your doorstep and keep them contributing to your profits and their portfolios.

The human capital drought is for real

Timelines to identify, source, interview, and extend an offer take longer now than they did three years ago. Plan your talent hunts early.

As of this writing, unemployment is 4.3 percent on average in the United States. Low unemployment, coupled with a shifting demographic relative to an aging workforce, has created a shortage of qualified workers. In addition, the younger workers, Generations X and Y, have a different work philosophy; they don't play by the same rules as the generations before them. Employees across the board are demanding higher compensation plans to switch companies and demanding more perks, and sign-on bonuses are being used more frequently. Hiring managers are under pressure to fill vacant positions quickly to avoid overloading other team members.

Healthcare, consulting, e-commerce, industrial, retail management, real estate, insurance, IT, software—you name it, there's a shortage of and challenge to secure talented human capital. Managers today are only now beginning to realize that the mature worker is just as competent and motivated to assume jobs that were historically offered to younger workers.

Research also proves that older workers are more loyal, stay with companies longer, are less likely to call in sick, are more willing to work overtime, and are more reliable and able to deal with complex customers and service issues. Even with the potential of higher healthcare costs associated with older workers, the additional costs, are offset by less turnover and lower training costs and recruiting fees.

Search professionals, human resources executives, and contract recruiters are also feeling the pinch of a tight labor force. The costs associated with sourcing, advertising, researcher pay, and direct marketing continue to rise, as well as the time needed to find the right talent for a specific organization. Don't wait till the last month of the quarter to call your favorite search professional to retain his or her for the executive you need by the end of Q3— you'll be under the gun to get the person that fast, and likely to make poor decisions just to get it filled.

The good news is that there are millions of bright and well-qualified executives out there who may be flying under your radar. You may be overlooking these candidates because their experience comes from a different field or industry. Your role as a creative executive—i.e., chief talent scout—for your company is to recognize and document the core competencies and skill sets needed for the openings in your company. Know these qualities, embrace and study unique talents in others, and you will be able to source from a larger pool of candidates.

Research continues to show companies without a solid training program and defined, up-to-date job specifications continually misfire in hiring talent that is best left working for your competition.

"I love you, Danny, but I can't marry you. It's the pigs."

from *Waking Ned Devine*

Check with a consultant to confirm your compensation plan ranks in your industry's top percentile. If not, change it.

In the quirky and hilarious film *Waking Ned Devine,* a small farming town in Ireland schemes to snooker the country out of the lottery winnings of a dead man. One of the stories in the film is the love between a pig farmer and a lady in town. She loves him but can't bring herself to marry him and live with the smell of a pig farm. Only when he gets the lottery dough and bids the farm adieu does she agree to marry him. Moral of the story: Why put your energy into convincing potential employees to join your firm when you don't pay a competitive wage?

Up the ante. Attract the better talent with better pay—not a lot more, but slightly more than the rest— just below the number one in your marketplace. See what happens. You'll reduce turnover (which will offset the cost increases of better pay plans), enhance morale, attract better talent, and rid yourself of making excuses. It also makes a bold statement to your customers that you want and expect the best. They won't object as much, either, when you raise your prices if you're doing a great job!

Speak the language of business clearly

Clarity of intention is the most important skill and habit you can use when interviewing candidates.

February 2007: Santa Cruz de Tenerife, Canary Islands. A clever pilot thwarted a hijacking by alerting the passengers in French (a language the gunman didn't speak) that he would throw the gunman off-balance with a rough landing, and that they should be ready to attack the hijacker. It worked. The pilot landed, slammed on the brakes, and then accelerated, causing the hijacker to fall. The passengers and crew threw boiling water in his face and beat him into submission.

The message here is clear: Use language that your potential employees understand and can relate to. Rehearse your message whenever possible and have assistants review for content, clarity, and bias. New candidates are in hyper-focus mode when interviewing. Every word, every interaction during the interview process is magnified—a natural human condition when in new surroundings and having to make a critical decision. Be sure it's in a language for all to understand, lest the message get misinterpreted and you lose a viable candidate because of the wrong message.

Are your interview questions legal?

Asking the right questions is critical to identifying great talent. Asking the wrong questions will land you in court.

Does it matter how old a person is? Does it matter what language he or she speak at home? Is it important where the person's parents were born? Is it important whether the person is married, single, or divorced? Inappropriate interview questions come from bad habits and ignorance of the law and rights of individuals against prejudice and bias. Discrimination suits clog the courts with thousands of cases and cost corporations millions of dollars because of one single question—an illegal one. Managers, HR professionals, and CEOs must be educated on exactly what are the boundaries of appropriate and legal interviewing practices. Recently, 25 CEOs of a cross-section of companies with revenues of $5–30 million were given a 20-question test of interview questions, and the CEOs had to answer "Proper" or "Improper." The results showed more than 60 percent got more than two wrong. Yikes!

Secure the counsel of your labor attorney and prepare a seminar, worksheet, checklist—whatever it takes to train every one of your hiring managers on the appropriate questioning. Test everybody on a regular basis and demand updates on changes in the law from your insurance carrier and attorney.

Hear ye, hear ye!
A radical proclamation

Announce and publish your policies, philosophy of business practice, and hiring process to the world.
Think "branding."

In our world of instant video journalism, blogging, message boards, and YouTube, your company's internal operations or issues are out there for all the world to see. If there is the slightest change in company policy or an internal conflict, rest assured, it will show up somewhere on the Web. Why not make the messages that leak to the public domain positive? As a corporate leader, it's imperative for you to convey clear messages to your employees. Write a clear mission statement, then post it everywhere—from the lobby to the company newsletter to the back of pay stubs. Have your marketing team write a blog post or post it to a job message board.

Let potential employees know what your company is really about—its philosophy and business practices. Rarely do you see this courageous approach to attracting new talent. All too often, companies spend big bucks telling what they can do for the customer, yet fail to effectively communicate ideas, goals, and encouragement to their own employees. This is all well and good, but it doesn't say anything to the potential and current employees about the philosophy of customer service issues, freedom to make decisions, or flexible pay options for sales and service people. There is nary a word about what good things will happen when an employee works hard and smart, and what will happen if he or she doesn't.

Be different! Let employees know how their hard work will be rewarded. And announce up front and out loud that employees will be fired if they don't do their work. A few of the newer, innovative technology firms have caught the wave and are benefiting from this candid and radically refreshing approach to hiring. Be radical! Tell it like it is!

Don't negotiate with a plumber on Christmas Eve.

Good talent is hard to find, and it ain't cheap.

A general manager told the story about the time his wife attempted an Oriental noodle recipe on Christmas Eve for their guests. At her request, he tasted it. She wanted feedback, so he offered his assessment: "Yuck!" She immediately dumped the entire contents into the sink, taxing the poor garbage disposal and creating a seriously clogged pipe.

Close to 8:00 P.M., he finally found a plumber. "Gonna cost you double, you know!" the voice challenged. "Tell you what I'll do," said the general manager. "I'll pay you two and a half times your fee if you're here in 30 minutes!" The plumber came and fixed the drain. Money well spent. Being cheap is a habit and one that won't serve you well if you're going after top talent. The American way of negotiation is: Make an offer, other party counters, first party counters the counter, they agree to split the difference, and the deal is done. Attracting great people with this approach won't work. Why? Because the top performers in every market know this game. They play it every day with their customers. They're good at it and don't have to play with you. Make a solid offer and be prepared to pay a premium for the best. If you need a person to start yesterday, now is not the time to try to save money. Your customers are feeling the lack of attention, and it will be hard to replace them. Remember the lesson our general manager friend learned: The plumber doesn't have to come out to fix your drain on Christmas Eve; you've got to convince him he can't afford not to come.

"...and, this coffin makes a neat go-cart chassis if you decide not to use it below grade!"

Be creative in selling the benefits of working for your organization!

If your company's product or service may be seen as "boring" to a potential employee, find a creative way to sell it. You spend thousands of marketing dollars for potential customers; why not use a little extra effort to sell potential employees? Sell the excitement of your product's application or who your customers are. Demonstrate to potential hires how your product contributes to the health of people, the impact on an industry, the new technology it holds, the future of the marketplace, the commission plan they will enjoy, the lack of strong competition in the arena, and so on. Show candidates there is more to your company's products and services than what they see on the surface. Everybody needs to feel strongly about the product or service they represent, so help them to see the possibilities previously overlooked.

Defining your competitive advantage to attract top talent

What you think is your organization's key advantage could be a me-too feature and benefit.

In Jaynie Smith's enlightening book *Creating Competitive Advantage*, she advocates the importance of being able to articulate precisely what your competitive advantage is in the marketplace. This advantage could be that your product or service is the fastest, biggest, tallest, most effective, tastiest, smoothest, and so on. The trick is to separate a feature or benefit from a true competitive advantage and be able to define with quantitative proof your claims are true. And this is the tricky part. Take, for example, the me-too statement a home builder might make, such as, "We care about our customers." "Blah, blah, blah," as Jaynie says. So does every other builder, right? Rephrase that statement with some research and data to say, "Eighty-five percent of our customers are from referrals." Wow—now it sinks in. Proof, not just an empty slogan or cliché. Ask "So what?" to test your advantage and see if it holds up to the scrutiny.

Test, measure, restate, test, measure, restate. Spend time reading Jaynie's fast and fun book. Test your mission statement and branding concepts to be sure there's an alignment with brand and advantage. If you can't state it, top talent will head to the companies that can define it clearly.

"He went for a smoke break and never came back!"

It's not always about the money. People change jobs for reasons beyond the almighty and alluring buck.

At a global conference in Los Angeles in the spring of 2007, an executive from a British consulting company shared a funny story of how difficult it is for him to hire and retain top executives and middle managers in the heart of India's business district. The executive explained how interviewers had to be excellent representatives of the firm and even better judges of talent—fast judges, as candidates are interviewed and offered the job often within two hours. If his interviewers didn't do a great job of selling the company, a person may take the job, show up for work the next day, and during a smoke break interview 10 floors above to secure a better deal from the competitor!

Your ability to attract top talent depends on your company's ability to be competitive in many arenas. In a survey a few years ago, a major corporation found that money was one of the top 10 reasons people took jobs, but it wasn't number one. More times than not, people

26

leave jobs because of their direct supervisor. In fact, other attractive factors included advancement potential, personal satisfaction, recognition (a feeling of worth and contribution), surroundings, professionalism, management style, commute time, and above-average pay for the work assignment. Money alone will not attract top talent. Ask candidates what factors will influence their decision to take or reject a job offer from you. If all else fails: Don't let anybody take a smoke break!

"Xanadu is over there, madam."

*Being candid with potential hires will go further
in securing them for your organization.*

If you own a gold mine, your most protected data are geological maps. When a gold mining company in Canada ran into low yields, it suspected the maps might not have been accurate, so, rather than hiding its secrets, it sent out a message to the business community offering a reward for additional information on where there may be gold on its land. The result? Seismologists, old-timers with folk tales and funky maps, amateur gold miners, and the like showed up to give whatever data and ideas they had to claim a potential reward. Empowering others to gain value instead of hoarding data that may be obsolete is a win/win.

Sharing classified information is not a sign of strength. Most people realize no company is perfect. All businesses—unlike the mythical, magical place called Xanadu—must deal with public and private issues daily. Each one has a unique cluster of issues, agendas, and pressures to face in an ever-changing market. Be candid with candidates. Explain in positive language what problems your company faces, what you're doing about them right now, and what you're planning to do in the future. Show them how they can contribute to the company to make it better. Show them where the ideas are coming from. And let them know they'll be asked for their suggestions if they become part of the team. Ask potential hires to offer suggestions, based on their observations, for improving the company's performance.

If your firm has had bad press lately, discuss it openly and candidly. Defend, but don't sell. Explain the issue as it relates to the industry as a whole. A client of ours, an environmental cleanup company, was great at attracting talent from its larger competitors. Why? Because it promoted the fact that the industry had big problems as a whole, but by working for a smaller firm, employees could make a greater impact on fixing the problem. It emphasized the difficulties large, slow-moving corporations can have with an overly cautious board of directors too scared to make the wrong moves. And it did attract top-flight talent who did make a difference! Remember: The bloggers are like gold miners: They'll dig, then write about what you're doing or not doing.

Brag about people who have left your company.

Admit it? YES!

Bragging about individuals who have left your organization can demonstrate just how well you train people to be superstars. Sharing the current successes of past employees shows that you hire and then support the best talent possible. Letting candidates see that they may learn a lot more than they expected at your company is essential to retaining top talent. Let them know that you want them to grow and you will continually challenge them in their respective roles.

Showcasing success allows employees to see that you will mentor them and help them grow. Then, if they want to advance, they must help find their replacement and mentor that person. In reality, people don't like to change jobs. We all like to be part of a successful team or family. Find ways to show that people can grow, prosper, be challenged, and be recognized within your company. And if they outgrow their jobs, they know they'll be very marketable in the business world having worked for you. Who knows? They may leave, open a business, and hire you as CEO and partner!

Retention is everybody's responsibility

Retaining the best of the best is an everyday event. Study what keeps people onboard at other companies and copy their habits.

The company behind Facebook, a dominant social networking site, provides three meals a day and laundry service for its 200 employees, according to a recent *Fast Company* interview with its co-founder, Mark Zuckerberg. Starbucks provides health insurance for part-time workers hitting the minimum hours to qualify. Wow! Wynn Resorts supports workers driving three hours to pick up a guest's medicine she forgot at home. "No special parking spots," was proclaimed by Terry Semel, former Yahoo! CEO, about the parking at the corporate headquarters. To reduce turnover and find hidden landmines in your organization, survey your employees' impressions of the work environment, start a dialogue with existing key executives to ensure conflicts are not being hidden, train them on effective interviewing skills to better screen for employees who fit the culture, and utilize competitive compensation and healthcare benefits. Taking a proactive approach to retention is critical to reducing turnover down the road.

Spend serious time reviewing the excellent research and leadership assessment and development provided by consulting companies such as Mercer Human Resources Consulting; Watson Wyatt; RHR International; AST Solutions, run by Dr. George Watts; Growth Solutions, LLC, run by David Fritz in Naperville, Illinois; among others. Their data and insights are fascinating and provide key ideas on how to position your company to retain top talent with factors other than throwing money at the problem.

MySpace…your space.
Whose space is it?

The success of social networking websites such as MySpace and Facebook is nothing short of phenomenal. MySpace has become the most popular social networking site in the world, with more than 95 million members. It accounts for 80 percent of all visits to online social networking sites, according to Wikipedia. Facebook has the largest number of registered users among college-focused networking sites, also according to Wikipedia. Equally amazing is the actual content published on the individual web pages of its subscribers. This information includes personal details about the subscriber, including photos, hobbies, links to friends, music, and other individualized content designed by the subscriber that projects an outward-facing virtual representation of whom that person wants the reader to see.

Many employers are using Google to research information on potential candidates to gain a better perspective of the candidates' personal tastes—or lack thereof. Some of this information can influence a hiring decision—or a termination! Since the information is in the public domain, anyone can see it, including co-workers, clients, and other professionals who may view the individual—and your company—in a negative light, depending on what personal information is found on the Internet.

Some candidates (and current employees) appear to be getting the message loud and clear, and are changing and deleting some or all of their negative content to appeal to potential and current employers, while others view this information as the way they want to be perceived by the rest of the world. Incorporate a Google search on potential candidates and current employees to see what's on their space. You may be surprised at the results!

Walk a mile in their shoes.

*Engage human resources personnel to work closely
with management and proven search firms in hiring
key executives. Get HR out in the field for
some close observations.*

Arrange for your HR staff to spend some time in the field. As they learn what managers see, feel, and do under real pressure-packed situations, they will be better able to spot a qualified candidate in the sea of résumés and Internet bios. It will also give them freedom to consider alternative backgrounds.

Also, as professional recruiters, if we can spend some time with managers from various departments, our success ratio goes way up when we're evaluating candidates for the job. Mandating that your managers spend time with your search firm partners will provide your partners a better picture of the culture and pace of the company. This approach, coupled with clearly defined job descriptions that include performance metrics and strategic goals, is the best insurance against making poor hiring decisions. Risk is reduced with good data and accurate observation. The good news is that it doesn't cost any more in recruiting fees.

Rapid reconnaissance to sharpen the image of your company and employee retention program

Four enlightening questions to ask every employee in the next week to validate your recruitment strategy:

- *What keeps you here?*
- *What attracted you to this organization?*
- *What concerns you enough to consider leaving?*
- *Who do you know who would want to work here?*

Ask these four questions through a confidential, no-names-anywhere questionnaire. Put this questionnaire into every paycheck envelope or with the employees' direct deposit statements once a year with a note from you stating why you're asking. Rapid reconnaissance, an expression coined by researchers, means "to gather data quickly to assist in making changes in a policy, method, or position." The media uses this tactic with opinion polls on busy street corners, through the Internet, and over the telephone. Why can't you?

The responses you collect could be candid or extremely ambiguous. However, they can provide insight and accurate feedback concerning hunches and observations, as well as some great referrals. These four questions will elicit varying responses; some may baffle you, others will surprise you, and the rest will teach you. You can use this data to direct how your firm presents itself to potential candidates during interviews, through advertisements, and on your website. Gather your staff and review these comment cards—no names revealed—and sort out the real issues from the inconveniences. And don't take any too lightly.

Encourage them to find another job? Well, sorta.

Parallel careers are here to stay. Embrace the benefits.

Employees who work full-time for you, and then are energized enough to have a small business or a hobby turning a profit, are typically bright, motivated people. The engineer who consults on the side, the plant manager who restores and sells antique cars, the marketing manager who builds doll furniture—all have talents they want to expand and share. CEOs and key executives are challenged in trying to measure a manager's loyalty to the company as it relates to that employee's outside interests and business pursuits. With today's costs of college, housing, and healthcare, more people than ever are looking to supplement their income with part-time ventures that not only make money but provide potential retirement work and financial security.

To discourage a person from this will do more harm than good, and the individual may leave for a more understanding employer elsewhere. (The exception is the employee who has an obvious conflict of interest or spends so much time away from the job that it becomes an issue.)

Be open to unique ways people try to get ahead, plan for retirement, pay for nice vacations, and create niches in the business community. Also probe to check for lack of training or boredom that could be driving these outside pursuits.

Run help wanted ads
with pizzazz!

Stuffy, boring ads draw stuffy, boring people.

In regard to advertising, the Internet has created tremendous opportunity in the way products and services are marketed. In the last 10 years, we have seen more creative marketing, giveaways, writing, ad copy, banner ads, and content to sell and market every possible product and service. People are used to being entertained, thrilled, and marketed to. Potential employees are no exception. In today's marketplace, they want a good reason to get up, fight traffic, and travel the globe three weeks every month. They want to have fun and…oh!… make lots of money, too.

When those potential employees look at job advertisements, they are evaluating your company based on the tone and spark of your ad. They are also looking for what they will be able to do at this job. Whether you are advertising through Internet job boards, industry newsletters and journals, or the newspaper, and you want to attract the management talent who might be reading the postings, write more creative ads. Rather than post the job's basic requirements in blah language, capture the reader's attention with questions like: Can you show me documented proof you're in the top 10 percent in the marketplace? What awards have you won? Show potential employees that you have a sense of humor and fun, that you mean business but still maintain a balanced and engaging workplace. Tell them how they will be able to contribute to the success of the company or how they can grow. Show them that you promote teamwork and accountability. Even consider taking the picture of your building off your website and put a picture of the faces that represent your company. People care more about faces and fun, not fancy lobbies and a pond in front.

You're fired!

Some employees will never attain the levels of effectiveness you need to succeed. They have hit the "intellectual glass ceiling" and you have to let them go.

One theory of human behavior suggests that people are motivated and behave according to self-setting limits of behavior and emotions. These behaviors and emotions are suggested to be as much genetic as they are learned as a result of environment. Individuals in the workplace differ in that some show genuine curiosity and drive to learn, experience and excel in new tasks, build new relationships, and embrace intellectual challenges. Others decide to take the path of least resistance, least amount of risk—either physical, emotional, or intellectual—and seek employment that provides a reasonable wage and benefits, and that's enough. It is the latter group that, when pushed to change, offered a promotion, or asked to adapt to new policies or supervisors, seek out new employment that will allow them to return to a safe haven of emotional and intellectual expenditure. Ahhh, out of the line of fire. They have hit the intellectual glass ceiling…and will continue this behavior until some extreme event, some life-changing experience shakes them from their cocoon of security and change can occur.

Such employees can be effective in jobs requiring simple, methodical, routine tasks. We need people in these roles, to be sure. When it comes to managers and key decision makers possessing these traits of complacency, however, companies are headed for disaster. You will have to make the hard decisions, and some of those employees either must change or you have to let them go. Removing non-productive employees is a sign of a mature and confident leader.

Complacency-minded individuals can be detected during the interview process. Interview carefully and seek answers and examples of behaviors that show a willingness that they have to extend themselves beyond their comfort level—either physically, emotionally, or intellectually—at various points in life. Prior company cultures, traditions, management philosophy and style will also be big clues in determining a fit in your organization. It is much easier to not hire someone who has already hit the intellectual glass ceiling than to have to fire him or her later.

Section II

**Who to Hire:
Chasing the Purple Squirrel**

*There is something that is much more scarce,
something rarer than ability.
It is the ability to recognize ability.*
—Robert Half

Chasing the purple squirrel

*A talented executive can transition and be
successful anywhere…that is a myth.*

When a new player in the copier industry
ventured into the American market in the
early 1980s, it lured—with big signing
bonuses and fat commission promises—management
talent and salespeople from established players like Xerox
and IBM. It worked. New recruits jumped from their
respective arks for the new kid on the block, yet they
failed miserably. Reason? The company discovered that
the managers and sales professionals selling a brand-name
product sold differently than those selling a "non-brand-
name" product. (Brand-name products are those that are
considered "household names." They have long histories
of dependability, celebrity endorsements, and fancy
advertising. Non-brand-name products are sold around
the concept "It's time for a change." These products offer
new features and introductory pricing, and are often
pitched as a backup to your existing product.) Once
management realized the old adage "A good salesperson
can sell anything" was a myth, they refocused recruitment

efforts to secure successful talent from the companies without a widely recognized brand. Result: Sales rocketed and that company is still in business today.

Chasing a purple squirrel refers to seeking an ideal job candidate who, in reality, does not exist. No one person has all the attributes, experience, image, and compensation requirements to fit a job profile. The key is to seek out people who can relate to your industry's business cycle, cost systems, delivery schedules, and manufacturing processes. If a person has experience and skills in an industry with similar practices, he or she should be able to adapt to your marketplace quickly. For example, a person managing a local bank should understand the management role in another financial services corporation. A manager in the hospitality sector should understand retail or another consumer industry. Someone in the freight business should be able to easily adapt to the automotive, railroad, or aviation industry. We've even witnessed numerous individuals leave the field of politics, becoming successful directors and operations managers because of their talent and experience in building teams and consensus.

If you are a purple squirrel chaser, stop now. Re-evaluate what you are really looking for this person to do in the job and evaluate him or her on prior experience and success—not on purple squirrel attributes.

Rattle the tree and shake things up

If you're interviewing new executives for your team, look for individuals outside the model of past hires. Look deeper for a trail of positive value to an organization or a history of shaking up the group, and bring 'em on board!

Often, renegades don't get hired because current executive leadership sees "high maintenance" written all over them. If you find people who don't fit the mold, don't discount them right away. Look at what they've accomplished in their lifetime. Can their unique, or even quirky, skills be harnessed and channeled into your company? Can they teach you something you don't know? Are you trying to create a new and vibrant culture? If these unconventional leaders have survived and received a paycheck from someone for years, they must be doing something productive. Dig deeper in your interviews. Conduct your own reference checks to probe for unique, even opposite, approaches to business practices and leadership development. Have them meet other members of your staff during the interview process to be sure there is a good blend of different personality styles.

It all goes back to having a good process of measuring specific traits and competencies. Differences are good. If you all think the same, why even discuss it?

Hire personality,
not just pedigree.

*Reforest your organization with hardy seedlings,
even if they don't have a lot of experience.*

G o into the corporate restroom and look yourself in the mirror. Would you have hired you when you were fresh out of school? Someone did. Why did they hire you? What spark, idea, attitude, energy did you exude to secure an offer without the experience they and everybody else said you needed to get hired? Those same traits are in others as well. Look closely for individuals with these qualities. They are out there!

Future billionaires wanted

*Starting out, Microsoft's Bill Gates didn't run ads
that read, "Must have Windows experience."
Hire those with histories of past successes.*

W hen you rewrite the job description, make
an effort to describe the job without using
the clichés of a basic job description. Instead,
use the job description to describe four to five key initiatives
that you will expect this person to accomplish in the next
18 months. Then be on the lookout for examples of similar
initiatives/experience in the candidate's background. If he
or she shows a history of success in completing short-term
objectives, continue talking with this person. S/he could be
the right "fit" for the role. Express in action words what the
job really is about, its core issues, what a person needs to
like to do, and what he or she might dislike about the job.
What kinds of customers will he or she call on? See if the
traits and characteristics of the job match other industries
as well, thus opening up a whole new arsenal of available
talent you never considered. Leaders and entrepreneurs start
early in life. They leave footprints and fingerprints all over
the business scene.

Bring the mad scientists on board.

If they've survived in business this far, they
must have talent. Find it and enhance it.

Mad Scientists are different from Renegades. You know Renegades will be a handful from the get-go. Mad Scientists, the really creative types, have far-out, futuristic ideas and are different from Renegades in that they may not have a long string of accomplishments, but their ideas may lead to the next iPhone. Young, inexperienced managers or managers lacking courage will usually lean toward hiring the "safe candidate" for a position. If the person doesn't work out, the manager won't be criticized for hiring him or her. But hiring a Mad Scientist will always raise the eyebrows of the "finger pointers" looking for you to screw up. Take a chance anyway.

Have you ever watched an award show? You get to see and hear the people behind the writing and creation of the most successful movies, plays, and TV programs. They never look and sound like you thought they would, or should, do they?

Look deeper into people's nature and skills—beyond their wild hair, their theories of evolution, or the Hummer vehicles they pulled up in. They may have secret talents you need now. Encourage your executives to look for the super-creative types and don't penalize them for hires that don't work out.

Gold watches are for train conductors, not for today's elite executives.

Candidates today take different tracks to get to their destination. Those who show numerous jobs early in their career show a willingness to take risks and venture out.

The days of the gold watch ceremony for the 20-year employee are history in our knowledge-based workplace. As our workplace continues to evolve into a project-oriented/performance-based employment arena, the necessity for a person to demonstrate long tenures at companies is not as important. And unemployment levels in the 5 percent range, coupled with a strong economy, have created the perfect storm of competition in search of human capital. The reality is that the executive who has worked for three companies in 15 years is more valuable and sought after than a person who has worked for one company for 15 years. Why? That individual has a broader band of experience and proof he or she can adapt to change. What's important is when the person worked at these different positions and what he or she did while there.

Quick job changes early in a post-college career are typically made out of naiveté, lack of direction, or a missing mentor.

Conversely, excessive jobs late in a career can show confusion and a lack of updated skills. Experimenting with a few different jobs can be a great lesson before a person sets firm with a company for many years. If the individual doesn't investigate other opportunities early, he or she will likely be curious later. Spend adequate time exploring the person's real passions and successful experiences in life outside work as well. Herein lie clues to what the candidate may be searching for in a career.

Does the job seat cushion spring right back up?

Look deeper when interviewing key executive candidates having more than six years with their current employer. Complacency and lack of motivation to excel could be present.

We all have a favorite chair at home. If you were to sit in someone else's, the chair would be uncomfortable. The cushions are now shaped to conform to the other's body, not yours. People stay in jobs with the same effect. Steady employment with one company is still looked upon as a positive. Loyalty and consistent performance are indeed important. However, if the long-tenured person has had the same job, has performed at the same level, and has been given only a few token promotions, then he or she is not the person you want to lead your group to the promised land. Former CEO Terry Semel, who left Yahoo! in 2007 after a career at Time Warner of nearly 20 years, admitted he didn't understand the space at all when he got to Yahoo!. It grew in a big, big way, although Semel left after the company felt it needed to take the business to a higher level to compete with Google.

In most cases, the person you hire to create dramatic change will not become a long-tenured employee. It is not in the nature of such personalities in business. If you need managers to implement change, be sure when interviewing to find out what they've been doing outside the workplace. Starting a family, getting an M.B.A., renovating houses, caring for a sick family member—all may show they have the drive to excel, but perhaps they haven't had the time or the opportunity to express it fully. Remember, loyalty and longevity are not the same thing.

Catch, release, and catch later.

Keep track of the upcoming superheroes.

Clever managers are always recruiting and networking. What if you don't have any openings? Don't worry, you will. In the meantime, when you meet young and dynamic talent who still require a few years of street-seasoning, keep in touch with them on a bi-yearly or yearly basis. Add them to a tickler file in your contact database or offer an informal mentorship. Toss them back in the business world pond and let them grow. Then put your pole in the water and reel. These young people are your future elite. Also develop a strong relationship with a search firm or two that understands your culture and vision and has proven it can identify talent who are dynamic enough for your organization.

I won't go and you can't make me!

*The potential employee who is not willing
to relocate isn't all bad. This attitude shows a belief
in stability and community. Loyalty and a sense
of community can be great client relations tools.*

Blended families, dual-income households, aging parents in need of long-term healthcare from family, and cost of living are all factors keeping people in their neighborhoods. Cultural differences across the country, and the effort to adjust to them, can also make it difficult for people to move, even for a great promotion. Allowing employees to remain local encourages loyalty and can even be good for business. Customers like dealing with a stable, long-term member of the community rather than a superstar on his way to another job. Many talented and balanced executives will no longer jump through hoops for unreasonable and unhealthy demands of overzealous managers. If relocation is not an option, try to find a win/win for everyone. Not only can you retain key talent, but it may help you retain key customers, too.

Consider hiring the number-two candidate.

Number-two candidates can be the unsung heroes.

Number-two sometimes is likable but doesn't have as much "industry experience" as number-one, so you pick number-one. If number-one is hard to pin down with an offer, shows signs of hesitancy in taking the job, makes unreasonable demands, or holds out for big bucks, hire number-two. That person wants the job more, will take it for reasonable pay, and is less likely to defect to your competitor. If you are still in doubt about your number-two, use this quick test to see who is the strongest: Have both candidates create a one-page strategic plan outlining their first 30–120 days on the job. Now let's see who really has ability and motivation to plan out his or her first days on the job. You'll find your top person in this simple exercise, and you may be surprised at your number-two.

Hire the disabled.

*The power of the human spirit should
never be underestimated.*

Millions of Americans with disabilities hold
down jobs, and they are darn good at what
they do. Keep your eyes and ears open for such
talent. These individuals are worth their weight in gold.
As technology has allowed a highly mobile workforce, the
ability for organizations to secure bright-minded and eager
workers into the fold has never been better.

One percentage point shouldn't stop you from buying a house.

*Don't wait for Mr. or Ms. Perfect to show up.
A little extra training of a solid candidate
will give you a superstar quicker than
waiting for one to magically appear.*

A candidate with a solid personality, strong education, and right attitude has the potential to outperform the talent from your competition who is asking for the sun, the moon, and the stars to change jobs. Taking one month to train, reading industry newsletters, and attending one trade show will get most managers up to speed. They can get the minor details and technical assistance from internal staff and you. Bottom line: Hire a solid person, and don't wait for Mr. or Ms. Wonderful. In our business community today, there's a simple mantra: If you like the candidate—someone else does, too. Hire his or her now!

Section III

How to Hire:
Soup, Salad, and Tons of Questions

*A single conversation across the table from a wise man
is worth a month's study of books.*
—Chinese proverb

Candidate interview question of the century

"What businesses did you start from the time you were eight years old through high school?"

Entrepreneurs and leaders start early in their quest to do something apart from the group. Find out what they did. We recently completed a search with a VP of sales who believed that every sales professional or sales manager who was above average in his or her profession started out early in business pursuits. This VP probed during the interview to see who shoveled snow from driveways, mowed lawns, worked at the grocery store, baby-sat, worked toward an Eagle Scout badge, or sold Girl Scout cookies. In college, did the candidate work in the cafeteria, paint houses in the summer, work as a lifeguard, or make and sell T-shirts with the school logo on the front? Demonstrated motivation to earn a living at a young age shows gumption and a willingness to work hard. They also demonstrate a desire and drive to become successful and financially independent. Test this theory out on your existing staff. Find out who of your staff was the most assertive in his or her youth and see if he or she is the most highly paid.

Emergency interview questions

Behavioral-based interview questions provide fast insight into understanding a candidate's history of success, thought process, and motivation.

Many organizations do not have a formal interviewing process. Rarely are there standard formats and templates for grading or addressing specific skill sets and traits to compare to the job specification. Research also shows that managers are given less training in effective interviewing strategies than than in other business topics. As a result, managers rely on old, outdated, and even illegal questioning approaches when interviewing key executives.

The following list includes proven questions that will elicit keen insights on a candidate's work history and success, thought process, and motivation. This is not an all-inclusive list; however, if you're stranded on a deserted island, or snowed in at Toronto airport, this list will serve you well in an emergency to determine if the candidate goes on to the next step.

- What questions do you have for me right away?
- What would really surprise me about you? What else?

- What reading material would I find on your coffee table, nightstand, kitchen table, or in your car?
- Tell me a story about you in an ethical dilemma and what happened.
- How did you earn money while in college?
- How far away from home have you traveled?
- Draw me a pie chart showing how you spend an eight-hour day.
- Are you a curious person? And, if so, show me an example.
- What's your favorite success story and failure story?
- What do you consider to be your biggest work-related success?
- What should I have asked you that I haven't?
- Want to be a millionaire? Why? What are you doing to prepare for the day?
- How would your world change if you made $35,000 more next year? Are you ready to resign from your job in five days? What will they do when you quit?
- Share some stories about the four most influential people you know.
- Have you ever created a strategic plan for your job or career?

- What is your philosophy on the subject of goal setting?
- Tell me how your management style helped someone grow.

Listen…very carefully.

It's how they say it that can make the difference.

One of our favorite stories is about a CEO who was interviewing a woman for a sales position with his firm. During the lunch interview, he was situated across from her and the sun was in his eyes, preventing him from seeing her face clearly. Rather than change tables, he sat and listened to her, discovering she had a captivating voice and energy. The job she was interviewing for required a lot of phone contact, and he knew she'd be fantastic with customers.

Too many times we are duped into believing image is more important than content. Words, passion, emotion, conviction, motivation, a history of success are far more critical than hiring image in an empty suit. Phone etiquette and energy are the big differences between an average sales professional and a superstar.

A good way to listen without the distraction of physical appearance is to speak with the candidate on the phone to see what impact the individual makes. The impression you get may more accurately indicate what he or she is really like. Attentive listening also shows genuine interest and

respect for that person, further enhancing the candidate's opinion of you as a compassionate, professional manager.

Read 'em like a book.

Ask candidates what three books they've read in the past year and what literature is on their coffee table at home right now.

In our excessive media blitz of advertising, 24/7 news, e-mail, and RSS feeds, we are bombarded with news we didn't ask for or continually being asked to spend money on things we don't really need. A person who doesn't read is no better off than a person who can't read. The real question to ask is: What do people pursue to read proactively? What people read is a view into their heart, soul, and interests. A person who doesn't read at least one book a month is at a distinct disadvantage with customers in social visits or negotiating. Keeping current with world events, business trends, creative thinking, and psychology has a direct correlation to personal income.

We recently interviewed a 46-year-old CPA/controller who admitted he hasn't read a business book or any writings about his field in the past 12 years. His income reflects his lack of effort to update his skills, and he is fearful of losing his job to a younger person. We wonder why. Reading and vocabulary are two signals to potential employers of the person's currency of skills and motivation to maintain a competitive edge in business.

CHOW CALL!

Meet with every candidate for hire at least three times, at different times and places each time. Watch them eat.

All of us have different peak energy times. Meeting a person once and deciding that the individual is not right for the job may be unfair—to you and to the candidate. If a person appears to have some potential but the "chemistry" isn't quite right, see the candidate again at another time of the day, and at a different location. People respond differently to the stress of a job interview. Some take longer to calm down or get more animated. Think back to how you interact with others, and give the candidate the benefit of the doubt if he or she is not perfect in the interview. Most people interview fewer than 15 times during their business career, so no one should be smooth and flawless. If a potential employee is, it should be cause for concern.

Finally, meet his or her for a meal. The act of dining out can show much about a person's social graces, health awareness, and conversational style. The event can be a great starter toward learning more about that person's lifestyle, goals, and other talents.

Dear John...

*Get a sample of any potential hire's writing skills
to verify an ability to communicate on paper.*

The higher an executive works in an organization, the more potential for speaking, writing, and appearing in the media. Just as phone presence is critical, a person's ability to communicate on paper is vitally important. E-mail, memos, and letters written by remote sales professionals go out to customers without any proofreading. Are you willing to take the risk of unprofessional and embarrassing letters? Have a potential employee write a sample letter to a customer for you. Have him or her send you a sample of a proposal recently mailed out. Ask whether the candidate attended college and whether English was a strong or weak subject. A good assistant can shore up weak skills in this area, so if the person is strong in other areas, he or she is not totally out of the running. But get the new hire a good grammar book and a dictionary in a hurry! Develop a questionnaire that is specific to the position the candidate is applying for. This will give you a very good perspective of both his or her writing skills and his or her thought process.

On psychological assessments

*Use tests to help you to manage and coach. Do not use them
as final decision-makers to determine whom to hire.
Reliance on assessment reports builds
weak interviewers and indecisive managers.*

Assessment testing has reached an all-time high
with the influx of Internet-based "quickie"
personality profiles. But many of these tests do
not have the validity, reliability, or company benchmarks
to make them useful other than for curiosity's sake.
Assessment profiles—even the best ones—should not
be used exclusively to pick a winner. In one study of over
more than companies, it was learned that about half of the
companies don't use any kind of psychological assessment
tools. Some studies have shown no major differences in
performance issues, lower turnover rates, or more frequent
promotions in companies that do use assessments.

Dr. Jean Piaget, the world-renowned researcher in
child psychology, performed studies that tested genius
in children. He found that if he changed the way the tests
were presented—written, verbal, question-and-answer,
or essay—different segments of the group showed genius.

In other words, different children were identified as geniuses using each of the different tests. The point is, people excel and learn by different methods, yet all have potential never tapped. Bottom line: Assessments are a great tool in interviewing. Use them as such without giving them the power of the final decision to hire or not. The key element that cannot be fully assessed is the potential of an inspired and motivated individual.

If you love lobster,
you'll pay market price.

When you find who you need, pay for value.

It's Saturday night and you're out with your spouse for dinner. You'll pay whatever the amount to satisfy your craving for lobster. The same principle applies to the search for talent. Good talent is always more expensive. Pay the extra. Don't try to secure top executives with weak salary offers. They'll leave if a better offer comes along or will resent your offer forever, even if they take the job. Research continues to prove that while people leave jobs for reasons other than money, they will not accept a new job without adequate compensation to offset the risk of leaving a sure thing. Offering a stronger incentive plan tied to performance will both entice real performers and instill a strong accountability component to the package. It's similar to the buyer who tries to negotiate with a vendor after her "favorite" vendor can't deliver the product. The buyer asks: "How much? Our other vendor sells it for $5 dollars per foot." The seller responds: "Then buy it from them!" Buyer: "They don't have any." Seller: "Well, when I don't have any, I sell it for $1 per foot!" If you have salary parity issues that preclude your hiring a new employee for a bigger salary even though the person is worth more than your existing talent, it's time to change the policy. You're penalizing yourself with mediocrity.

The definition of insanity

Have you ever heard that doing the same thing over and over while expecting different results is the definition of insanity? Are you hiring a person who fits a mold, or someone who can make a difference?

The banking industry always complains about how difficult it is to hire and retain bank tellers. Why? Because a teller job doesn't pay well. The banking industry also says it's the most important job because tellers meet the customers all the time. Yet the industry refuses to pay a better wage! Why? "Because it's always been that way." Insanity! No wonder banks can't afford to pay better interest rates on our savings accounts and chain their pens to the table. It costs them too much to keep retraining these so-called important people.

If you have constant problems filling a tough position, reconfigure it to fit a wider berth of available talent—and pay better than the going rate or offer other incentives that make the position more attractive. A few years ago, a major fast-food chain lost millions of dollars as the result of a very successful toy giveaway promotion. The promotion cost it thousands of employees who quit from burnout and excessive hours because the company didn't consider the added strain on and energy required of the employees. The company had to pay thousands of dollars to replace and train the employees who left. Hire talent and pay for what you expect.

Headhunters are not miracle workers.

Using three or four professional recruiters for one search is generally not the answer to filling a tough position.

In fact, using multiple recruiting firms for the same search assignment is actually counterproductive for a variety of reasons. First, most executive search firms categorize each search assignment based on whether the search assignment is retained, partially retained, exclusive, or pure contingency. Generally speaking, most firms list pure contingency searches the lowest on their priority list and will work on those types of searches after finishing higher-priority engagements. Secondly, candidates become confused in the search process when they receive two to three phone calls in the same week (or sometimes on the same day!), further confusing them as to why any company needs multiple firms to fill the same search. They often wonder, "What's wrong with the position or the company?" Finally, candidates perceive some form of retained search assignments as a signal from the company that this search is important, and "…if someone is calling me, I must be important!" Next time, pay your search firm a retainer and you will notice a huge difference in the way both the candidates and the recruiters perceive your search assignment.

...you don't say?

Always do reference checks.

MIT, the prominent East Coast college, recently took some embarrassing heat when its longtime dean of admissions was discovered to have lied about having numerous college degrees. One simple call will verify, so what went wrong? Somebody trusted data without verifying it. Qualitative research has shown that more than 70 percent of hiring managers don't perform reference checks. Frightening! Reference checks confirm impressions and educate you on how to motivate, train, and discipline the new hire. Reference checks extract pieces of personal information that can clarify a feeling or hunch you have about that person, saving you from making a bad hire. References typically compliment the potential employee, but good questions can elicit surprising and relevant information.

We called a reference who told us (thinking this would help the candidate) the candidate was a workaholic and had been known to abandon his family at parties to rush to the rescue at the plant. No offer was made. Don't hire without making at least two reference checks yourself.

If candidates claim they can't give any references for risk of their company finding out they're looking, don't hire them. Ever.

Cementing the hire...
with chocolate?

*Flowers or a small gift to the spouse and
a solid offer are your best insurance against
a counteroffer being considered.*

Spouses of job candidates carry more influence than we imagine. They are not only sounding boards for your candidates; they make subtle observations and gain impressions from what the potential employees choose to tell them. If the opportunity is out of their comfort zone, spouses can deflate a deal in no time. A gift with a note helps to put a caring person behind a cold offer letter and a lot of inconvenience. A phone call to the spouse is not a bad idea, either (with the approval of the candidate, we suggest). However, pretty presents are not to be used to mask a weak offer or a job that won't be there after the first quarter.

Held for ransom

Never negotiate against a counteroffer. Never.

Rule number one: Avoid counteroffers. Discuss the potential of a counteroffer with a candidate on the very first interview. This upfront discussion allows you to prepare the candidate should a counteroffer be made and also discuss how he or she might handle the situation early on. Not only will it give you ammunition later on in the interview process, it will give you a good indication of whether or not he or she wants to make a change. Once you make an offer to a candidate for employment and have negotiated the final number, that's it. Tell the candidate, "This offer will not be negotiated should you come back to us once your current employer has countered with a better deal. We will not be used as leverage." Should the candidate come back with the comment, "Well, my current employer has offered to increase my pay, give me a promotion, and sealcoat my driveway for life, but I want to work for you. Is there any way you can match my company's offer?" Your response is simple and succinct: "No, we can't." You may feel like adding, "If you still want to work for it after you've blackmailed it into giving you what we know you're worth, but it didn't have a clue until today, then go ahead. And good luck." But don't say it!

Being held for ransom is dangerous and manipulative. Don't look with disfavor just yet on your candidate for using this tactic. Many people get bad advice, feel guilty for quitting, are unsure of its fairness, or have a touch of buyer's remorse. Hold firm to your guns and wait for an answer. Eight out of 10 times, the candidate will come to work for you with this approach.

Beyond a handshake deal

Always send a letter confirming your offer of employment.

People forget. Put details in writing, and we mean everything. Offer letters allow future employees to resign from their other job because they know your job offer is real; they will have a job after they go through the sometimes difficult separation from their current position. We advise all candidates to hold off resigning until the details of the offer letter are completed. A tangible letter diminishes the appeal of a counteroffer. Your future employee will be more committed to your organization because you put it in writing. "We want you!" Human resources should have an offer letter template and new hire orientation packet ready to mail out immediately upon a verbal offer commitment.

Section IV

**Managing and Retaining Elite Talent:
Business at the Speed of Change**

*When you hire people who are smarter than you are,
you prove you are smarter than they are.*
—R. H. Grant

Can you tell the difference between virtuoso and average?

Geniuses sit in chairs in front of computers and speak to customers every day. Do you know who they are?

As an experiment, Joshua Bell, one of the most renowned violinists in the world, donned a baseball cap, sweatshirt, and jeans, and headed out onto the platform of the Washington, DC, metro station at 7:51 A.M. on a Friday. He played for 45 minutes, earned $32 in change thrown in his open violin case, and never drew a crowd of more than a few passing commuters. Some of the commuters might have seen him, just three days earlier, when he'd played at the Boston Symphony Hall, where the cheap seats were $100. Do you really know the genius in your team? What can you do to better understand, listen to, evaluate, challenge, test, measure, or extract the talent that lies within each employee?

At your next management meeting, ask your top managers to make a list of what they think they're great at—work-related or otherwise. Have them share it with the group. Where can this "genius" make your company better? See what you learn.

Feelin' good and feelin' wealthy

*Put intrinsic and extrinsic rewards
in place for all personnel.*

Make sure you (or your assistant on your behalf)
make a regular practice of sending thank-you
notes and giving employee-of-the-month
awards, achievement pins, and commendation letters to
your employees. These special touches all point to
everyone's intrinsic, deep, need to feel appreciated. Your
team may be accustomed to the extrinsic rewards of base
salary increases, bonuses, vacations won in a sales context,
or a primo parking place for a great month. However, the
intrinsic rewards show a true level of appreciation. If you
really want to go the extra mile, give out appreciation
awards to a handful of employees at the next meeting or
town hall event. There's nothing like making someone feel
like a star in front of his or her peers. Try it and see how
it improves morale and employee retention. Remember:
Research shows people leave jobs because they don't like
their supervisor.

Live and die by the 80/20 rule.

*Prioritizing and targeting larger customers is crucial
to keeping morale high and employees informed.*

Vilfredo Pareto would have been a great sales manager. The late-19th-century Italian sociologist formed an economic theory—the Pareto theory—that basically says 20 percent of your customers will account for 80 percent of your revenue and 80 percent of sales made come from 20 percent of your sales force. Find an Internet connection and reacquaint yourself with the 80/20 theory.

At your next meeting, remind your team of this principle. Discuss the fact that the same amount of effort is expended on a big deal as on a small sale, so it's time to reevaluate their pipelines of business. Walk away from deals that don't fit the metrics you've already determined to be the best. Your staff will love you for it. There are things you and your team can focus on for more profitable business. Set minimum sales orders, seek advanced sales training programs, invest in market research to uncover customers that are bigger and in need of your products or services, raise the commission rate on larger orders, and see how quickly your orders get bigger overnight. Teach the staff you don't have to start at the bottom and work up. Be prepared to start at the top. Get a poster that has the 80/20 rule written on it, post it in your office, and see what happens.

Overcoming technical denial

All personnel must be able to turn on a computer, find the word processing program, and type and print a letter. If not, they don't go home until they can.

Pretty basic stuff, right? Some of your older employees may have an aversion to this "new technology," and your productivity will suffer as a result. There's no excuse. Offer a basic computer skills training class to all of your employees—next week! Make sure everybody can run the key programs needed to do their job effectively. Even if your personnel don't use computers every day, they must know the basics. In addition to increasing productivity, you're giving employees a safe environment to learn a new skill—a skill that now becomes a benefit to working for your company. Your employees will appreciate your generosity.

Paperwork costs profit dollars.

Limit weekly reporting or logging-in time
to less than three hours per week.

K ey executives are action-oriented. Give them tedious tasks and they will bolt faster than you can blink. Your top talent's DNA is coded for action and achievement. They're trained early that idle time is bad, that paperwork takes time away from managing, and that selling is productive. Consequently, you need to keep reporting methods to a minimum. Reconfigure your reporting systems to make them foolproof. Make it easy for executives to log their data and get back to productive work. Another option: Hire a few lower-salaried administrators to input data rather than forcing your revenue producers to do it.

Journey to the center of the girth.

*Offer an $800 yearly health club allowance and
an $800 continuing education allowance.
Make it a "use it or lose it" policy.*

Yes, people should stay fit, stop smoking, reduce
alcohol consumption, learn to control stress, and
consume less fat, but not all of us do. Sometimes
we just need a "nudge in the pudge" to get started. And
yes, we should all be lifetime learners, but that, too, is
easier said than done. Encourage your team members to
take time to practice healthy activities and challenge their
minds. By giving them a health or fitness allowance, they
can use the stipend on the healthy pursuit of their choice.
They may resist at first, but if you set an example, it may
turn them around. Don't forget to let your employees
know that if they choose not to use this allowance, they'll
be explaining why they haven't to you.

Schedule your next meeting on the ski slopes of Aspen.

Who knows what ideas will come up when you think outside the box?

Meeting with your team on a 11,200 foot mountain is a unique venue that can't help but do great things for creative thinking and team building. Boardrooms and meeting rooms stifle creative thinking through lack of stimuli and lazy habits. Sit around the fire of the chalet, have a snowball fight, and keep a pen in your jacket. Let the ideas flow! Consider other venues for your next meeting—Starbucks, the mall, the train station, in an RV on the way to a baseball game—something different that will bring out ideas and personalities you never see in your employees.

Laugh and sing your way to the bank: Innovative training programs are a must in today's business world.

*Seek out professional trainers and speakers who utilize new behavioral science, unique business data, and creative ways to deliver information.
Say no to PowerPoint presentations and flipcharts!*

We all know having fun while learning enhances retention and recall, and engrains that learning into our actions. Humor has the same effect. Music, too, activates different parts of the brain and limbic system and enables our minds to absorb and retain large blocks of information that drive changes in behavior.

Companies that implement innovative and unique programs for their employees have a better chance of both retaining and securing more employee referrals for new workers as a result of the company's willingness to escape conventional and boring training, as well as fancy motivational programs that have much rah-rah, but little substance and science behind the program.

Golden handcuffs for newcomers

*Create a "Retention Bonus Club": a percentage
of the employee's compensation to be paid after
three to four years of employment.*

When a worldwide manufacturing conglomerate was experiencing high turnover in its sales ranks, it elected to conduct a simple experiment with the sales team. It announced a stay bonus equal to 50 percent of one year's salary if a person was with it four years, starting from the moment the opportunity was announced. The result? Turnover receded, and, not curiously, performance of the salespeople increased.

It could be hypothesized that the salespeople wanted to ensure they didn't get fired before the big payout date. The increased sales more than paid for the stay bonuses and made it difficult for competitors to lure its people away with the almighty buck. (Interestingly enough, one of the vice presidents who was thinking of quitting before the stay bonus was introduced decided to stay for a while. Four years later, the company was for sale and he, along with four other executives, bought the company, making him a millionaire overnight. And yes, they still paid out the bonuses to the people who had earned them prior to the sale.)

Paying a stay bonus to a proven sales rep or manager after three or four years of employment is a lot cheaper than replacing that person after two years. Golden handcuffs do work, and they work both for the long and short term. Implementing a financial incentive will retain good employees, as long as the management team is fair, honest, and progressive. Money can't buy you loyalty, but it will buy you consistent performance in sales, as well as time to fix any internal glitches you've discovered. Advertising the program in the company newsletter and promotional pieces to the general public isn't a bad idea, either.

This joke's on you.

Laugh it up! Research shows it's productive, healthy, and good for business.

Has your staff seen you laugh in the past few days? Too busy to laugh? Are business demands so intense that it's difficult to see humor in a situation? Are you concerned your chuckles may indicate vulnerability and a weak presence in the business community? Hogwash. People are skeptical of business leaders who don't have a sense of humor. Laughing is a universal language, a sign of acceptance and spontaneous feeling. It is a tension reliever and offers a big breather in an important meeting. Sitcoms on TV even have to encourage us to laugh with laugh tracks; it's as if some of us need written permission to giggle. You will attract and retain staff far longer with humor and sincere efforts than with an iron fist. We heard of a president who purposely sat on a whoopee cushion at a meeting to ease the tension. Do you dare?

Excuse me, but that's my nose, not the pencil sharpener.

Hold all executive staff meetings in tight quarters.
Closeness encourages interaction.

Attention, assured managers! Never sit at the head of the table. Park yourself right in the middle. Invite others to sit closer to you and change the mix of who sits where. This ain't church. Move around. Break stale habits. Insist that everyone sit within arm's distance of their fellow comrades. We heard the story of a small company where the two big shots always sat at opposing ends of a long conference table. Employees on either side of the table couldn't see the reaction of both big shots at the same time, so the big shots could subtly communicate secretly during the meeting. Employees felt that trying to talk to both of them at the same time was like watching a tennis match from three feet away. The seating arrangement resulted in frustrating and confusing meetings. The tighter the space, the more ideas take place. Big tables, big rooms, and wide berths breed quiet and reserved dialogue. Being close together, sharing food, passing stuff to each other, and mingling with management does wonders for good communication, faster meetings, and a better exchange of ideas.

Hold your next sales meeting in the hall.

You'll probably resolve most issues there, anyway.
Try holding meetings in the bathroom,
if you want more privacy than the hall.

It's happened to all of us at some point. We realize the formal meetings are corporate cheerleading drills staged for the shareholders or the marketing people to show off the new ideas with much fanfare. Your time is valuable, and there's no need to be there for eight hours, so you finish your business in the hall in 15 minutes. Why not hold your next meeting there? People think faster on their feet. They appreciate the value of time. Try this informal setting next time you need to have a non-confidential meeting. See what happens.

Cast away, lad, into the great wide open.

Mandate a three-week sabbatical every two years for all senior management staff. No phone calls allowed. No exceptions.

Bill Gates disappears for more than a week to a cabin in the middle of nowhere just to think and review ideas submitted to him by his employees. Why not you? New ideas come while people are sitting on tractors, lying on beaches, hiking mountains, hitting the par-five in two, shopping in Paris, building a screened porch, antique hunting in Maine, or wandering the castles of Scotland. Reward your managers with free time—paid, of course—to do nothing but have fun. No rules, no suggestions. They must simply disappear to a place where you can't find them. It's amazing what ideas they'll come back with as well as a heightened sense of loyalty to you and to the company.

We find that if we don't take a few long vacations throughout the year, our performance is not as good as it could be. There are the shades of self-importance ("The world won't run right if I'm not here to hold the wheel");

worrying about missing some piece of business; or anxiety, not feeling as if we have "done enough." These feelings dissipate with R&R. We find that the business doesn't go away; if anything, more comes to us. It also shows our clients and associates that we are not "all business" and we care enough about our health and our families to take time off.

Go on, tell me. I can take it.

*Create a "customer evaluates us" form and
pass it out by next Monday.*

There's a lot of talk about value-added services these days; however, we have found that the majority of companies don't survey their own customers on a regular basis. Create a survey today to find out what your customers think of your products, customer service, interaction, and marketing. There are plenty of online resources to create and send surveys fast. Send it out today. What you find out will surprise you, scare you, thrill you, anger you, and motivate you to do things differently when you get up tomorrow.

Trash your favorite
beat-up slippers.

*Effective immediately: 15 percent of yearly sales must
be "new business," uncovered within the last 12 months.
Next year: 20 percent.*

A new contract or client increases profits. Older, established business keeps the machines running, inventory going out the door, and the bills paid. However, old business is generally performed at a lower price and with outdated expectations. And your older business will go away someday—you just don't know when. A constant stream of new clients and new business is insurance that you won't get blindsided if your established customers take business elsewhere. Make sure you have strong incentive plans for your management and sales teams to grow business. Your three- and five-year strategic plans should outline strong expectations for new business development and have written goals that are able to be tracked, measured, and rewarded for attaining. If not, you may not be in business in three to five years.

And the winner is...

*Create a "Nobel prize" for the top two
or three ideas of the year.*

Executives have all seen the power of sales contests during which people have worked five and 10 hours a week extra to win a $1,200 television, whereas the same energy exerted in non-contest periods would have earned them $20,000 in additional income! We've all seen reality television shows dishing out big prizes to those willing to join the fun. Appoint a project team of your most creative employees to design quarterly contests for your employees. The wackier, the better. They're great motivators and stimulators of teamwork and creativity. Have a few prize months per year and watch the sparks fly!

It's midnight. Do you know who else knows where your customers are?

Do you know the names and locations of your top seven competitors? Stop reading and find out now.

Isn't it amazing that with the vast Internet resources and competitive intelligence on the free market today, more than 60 percent of the candidates who sell or manage can't identify their company's key competitors? At your next sales or management meeting, make a point to discuss the competition. Ask for the list and see who knows and who doesn't. Discuss strengths and weaknesses and how they impact your marketing models and sales presentations. Equip your team with knowledge and you might sleep better at night. Better yet, hold a contest among the team: The one with the best data wins a getaway weekend to somewhere exotic.

If you build it, they'll read from it.

Create a "Library of Achievement."

reate a library of the top 20 business management, leadership, and sales books and audiobooks and keep them in your office for your employees to use. Have an assistant administer the borrowing process. Having a library that rotates the best material on business and selling throughout your workforce will do wonders toward enhancing sales, building team spirit and customer satisfaction, and building wealth for you and your employees. Start with some of the best authors: Brian Tracy, Harry Paul, Steve Lundin, Jim Collins, Denis Waitley, Ken Blanchard, Tom Peters, Marshall Goldsmith, Neil Rackham, Peter Drucker, Warren Bennis, Harvey Mackay, Stephen Covey. Contact Nightingale-Conant Corporation in Chicago for its catalog; it's the largest producer and distributor of sales training and motivational audiocassettes and CDs in the world; The Teaching Company is also an excellent provider of lectures on a broad topic list.

"Mr. Toobusy...please pick up the white courtesy phone. Paging Mr. Toobusy."

All calls to you from your team in the field should be returned within two hours.

If you're the boss and your employees can't get your attention, they'll leave to be appreciated somewhere else. Arrogance and claims of being "too busy" won't cut it as an excuse to leave a professional without a return call. Cell phones and PDAs are all perfect for getting timely data and details to all of your staff. Implement a time policy for return phone calls for your sales team, your management team, and yourself. Make sure your employees announce this return call policy in their voicemails. Statistics show the majority of managers don't leave because of money but because of perceived lack of appreciation and respect from their boss. Conversely, set limits on response times in late evenings and weekends. Our global workforce is only now beginning to challenge our once-precious evenings and "free time" on weekends.

Show me the money!

*Inquire about the existence of a savings or retirement plan
for every salesperson and manager in your group.*

A recent article in *The Wall Street Journal* showcased research indicating that intelligence is not necessarily correlated with financial success. One theory suggests that intelligent people take more risks with their money, even though they don't really have the skills to invest. Sadly, a high percentage of Americans do not have a regular, systematic savings program. Even corporate dollar-matching 401(k)s are not used by all workers. Sit down with your employees or hire a financial consultant for the day to speak with the team and explain the value of 401(k)s, stock plans, mutual funds, and certificates of deposit (CDs). Help them appreciate the feeling of having money in the bank. You are providing them with tools they can use long after they've left your company.

Setting employees' sights on financial independence shows them what they can do if they earn more: lifestyle changes, vacations, opening up their own business someday after they've outgrown their existing job.

You can be a hero to people who have never received any coaching on the topic of investing.

"That's a nice suit.
Does it come in your size?"

*Hire an image consultant for the day for all staff in view
of the public while representing your company.*

In the past 15 years, Russ's co-workers have cut two
neckties from around his neck and they've seen to it
that one of his coats disappeared. They were right in
doing it, too. Today's e-commuters don't need to get out
of their jeans to make a presentation; however, senior
executives are in the firing line of image and reputation.
Many professionals have forgotten or never learned what
a clean, professional image looks like.

For less than $800, you can teach your staff how to
dress for success—what colors to wear, styles to
complement body type and social expectations, hairstyles,
hygiene, and so on. Most people are never taught how
to dress effectively for business, the appropriateness of
certain clothing, or what colors and styles flatter a person's
physique. It will make a difference. It will make a
statement to your team that you're committed to hiring
the best, and having the best look their best.

Park the pink Cadillac out back.

*Remove all reserved parking, except for visitors
and handicapped.*

Two different views: The CEO of Yahoo! insisted on everybody having equal rights and no big favorites in the parking lot. Billionaire Steve Wynn, of Wynn Resorts fame, insists he earned it and expects the pampering of earned success, but treats his employees well in other ways. Reserve the primo parking space for the top salesperson, the customer service representative with perfect quality scores, or the person who had the best idea of the week. Reserve the limousine to take the group to lunch after a great quarter. Status symbols are great to give, not to show off to the team. People work harder for you if you reward them, not intimidate them.

To belch or not to belch:
That is the question.

*Take your team to international
etiquette school for a day.*

Do you know how to accept a business card from a Japanese businessman? Did you just toss your gum out the window in Taiwan? Uh-oh. Would you know if you just offended a foreign customer at lunch by not belching? In our global marketplace, it pays to spend a day with a consultant specializing in international business and etiquette training. Most of the major corporations in America provide some form of training for their employees who travel abroad. And fortunately, it's not expensive. A consultant for a full day could be less than $1,500. That's a bargain! One faux pas at lunch or the negotiation table could cost you 10 times as much. This type of progressive thinking speaks volumes to your team about being the best, as well as showing respect for clients by attempting to learn and understand their customs and traditions.

Required reading

Have your employees read and commit to memory the strategies from some of the best business authors today.

As an employer, you have the right to expect your staff to read anything you ask them to, within reason. Everybody needs to be on the same page when it comes to customer contact, selling skills, marketing, goal setting, hiring, and performance reviews. Some of our favorite books include:

Topgrading. Since 1999, *Topgrading* has been the number-one bestseller of more-than 1,400 books on employee selection and hiring. Bradford Smart provides an in-depth process and methodology for hiring, coaching, and keeping top talent. According to Smart, only 25 percent of those hired by Fortune 1000 companies turn out to be high performers, whereas Topgrading companies enjoy 90 percent success.

In Brian Tracy's book *The Psychology of Achievement,* he shares a wealth of knowledge and proven strategies on personal development for anyone who wishes to achieve more out of their his or her and his or her business. Tracy's goal-setting strategies have been taught to millions of people all over the world, and his no-nonsense approach to achieving whatever you what to be, have, or achieve is simply outstanding.

The book *SPIN Selling* by Neil Rackham, even though it was written nearly 20 years ago, is a great way to get people's minds moving in the same direction, creating a positive attitude toward the customer contact process.

Secrets of Great Rainmakers, by Jeffrey Fox, is a must read by everyone on your sales and marketing teams. Fox provides real-world strategies on how to take your business to the next level with proven sales and marketing techniques that drive new customers to your door while providing a roadmap of how to grow sales year after year from your existing customer base.

Musical chairs

Everybody changes places for a day or for one meeting.

How would you react if the boss changed the commission plan in midyear, and it cost you big bucks? You probably wouldn't be too happy. As the boss, you know material costs have risen 49 percent in two months, so to offset the costs you need to cut the auto allowance and overtime pay, and reduce air travel for your technicians. But how would your employees know that? What does it feel like to run a project management team, answer customer service calls, or work on the warehouse floor? Put people in different positions for a day to "walk a mile in the other person's shoes." If you let others know the issues you and other members of the organization face, they will be less apt to criticize, more likely to appreciate others, and more likely to accept decisions that affect their lives. This kind of openness builds a real team.

Let go of the leash.

Eliminate regular weekly meetings for the staff. If you need to gather the flock for a count, you lack trust in the group and it shows. Let them do their job or let them go.

Rah-rah meetings, Monday morning java, and jumping jacks are dinosaur tactics to motivate talented knowledge workers. Motivating a person to achieve a specific objective is accomplished by a one-on-one approach to evaluation of goals and objectives— either via phone or e-mails. Too many regular meetings per month scream that you don't trust that your workers are capable of doing their job without supervision. Unless you're a retail store that's meeting to discuss new merchandise, or a restaurant that's meeting to discuss daily specials, halt the meetings. With the time saved, you may actually see productivity increase.

Accountability day

December 15: Every salesperson turns in a résumé.

In *Search of Excellence* author Tom Peters defines a résumé as your "signature." Your résumé is a way to see immediately what you've been doing for the past year. This is pretty edgy stuff here, but it will send a message to your team that you care about what happens and are willing to work hard to deliver value. What better way to see in print what your group has done? Writing a yearly résumé forces them to prove they've actually been working the past 12 months. It's a great exercise to help marginal performers reach new levels and let superstars set higher goals and prove they're ready to be promoted. It gives a wake-up call to those who just won't make the cut to start looking for another job.

By encouraging your people to write their résumés, you're showing your team you're an innovative leader. You're building loyalty and a positive environment, and demonstrating your courage and willingness to help them advance or improve. Salespeople will leave at some point regardless of what you do or how much you pay. Helping the individual prosper and look good on paper is rewarded with loyalty and a desire to improve performance. And, by the way, don't forget to write your own résumé.

Philanthropy for the amateur

Provide a philanthropic budget of $500 to $1,500 per year for all managers with accountability for more than five people. Allow them to choose the charity and give the money in their name as well as the company's. Better yet, give them a day off to help a charity of their choice.

B
enevolence is very rewarding. Give your employees the opportunity to experience the heartwarming feeling of giving to others. This exercise goes a long way toward developing their "charity consciousness." It also speaks highly of your firm's commitment to humanitarian issues. Even a small amount of money (or time) can make a difference to someone, and you'll be promoting the practice for others to follow. Philanthropy is not reserved for the rich; it is an equal opportunity action.

Section V

**Staying Sharp:
What Got You Here,
Won't Keep You Here.**

*The key to becoming successful is to work
harder on yourself than on your job.*
—Jim Rohn

Continuing education for the CEO is ongoing

Set specific goals for each quarter around education in interviewing strategies, negotiating, Internet marketing, demographic shifts, rapid reading techniques, global technology, and so on.

Business models are being turned upside-down every day, disrupted by ever-advancing technology. Delivery of information to our doorstep, cell phone, laptop, television, radio, and the like is coming at us at light speed, so the busy CEO must be prepared to sort through ideas fast. Continuing education is the answer. Relearning how to become more efficient and a fast reader, for example, will pay huge dividends by being able to devour large amounts of reading material in half the time. Behavioral-based interviewing techniques will sharpen your skills to better identify top human capital from sources your competition hasn't thought of exploring. Health and nutrition education will provide you and your team better diet and exercise plans to stay healthy in hectic and high travel requirement positions.

Mandate that each member of your management team—and you—attends a minimum of four programs per year on a variety of topics delivered by an expert in the field.

Accountability: Who holds you accountable for decisions?

*Create or update your personal advisory board
if you own your own firm.*

Entrepreneurs are a unique breed. Some are driven to succeed, to invent, to sell, to build companies, to change the world, to disrupt the marketplace with upside-down ideas (think FedEx Kinko's, free AOL online e-mail, Starbucks' $5 cup of coffee, buying diamonds online).

Other entrepreneurs are more conservative. Perhaps they grew up in the family business or inherited it and took it to the next level. In both cases, the CEO is not responsible to report to anybody. He or she owns the place. Period. Most CEO entrepreneurs eventually create a board of directors or an advisory board to help make better decisions, brainstorm, define and install policies, and the like. Where are you in this stage of your career? Are you the boss and flying solo? Do you have a trusted advisory board who challenges your decisions and actions? Do you ask for constructive and direct criticism, or is your board a bunch of friends who come for the free dinner each quarter? Can you take the heat if they say you're nuts when proposing a change of some kind?

Independent research of business owners who are members of Vistage International, the world's largest CEO membership organization in the world, has shown that members grow their businesses faster than those who are not members. And while Vistage International is not the only organization that provides advisory board services and accountability, the fact is clear: Advisory boards protect and maintain good policies, double-check CEO decisions, and help align both corporate and personal goals for leaders. Examine your policy and approach to how you're growing and managing your organization. Do an analysis of how you view, make, and act on decisions in your day-to-day operations. Check out Vistage International as well, to learn more about its successful model of helping CEOs throughout the world.

Hello? Anybody home?

Personally contact any customer who was doing business with your firm a year ago but is not doing so today.

I f you're the boss or a sales professional new to the office, calling former customers can bring healing to those relationships. Letting customers vent their frustrations, disappointments, whatever, can help you reconnect with them if you want to. Customers go away for a lot of silly and vague reasons…and for some very serious and unchangeable reasons. Finding out why they left and wooing them back is worth spending a week calling around the holidays. Try it.

Never stop seeing customers.

Out of sight, out of business.

Whether you own the place in hometown USA or run a global organization, visit with customers. Let them see your commitment to their needs. Don't do your sales team's job, just visit. Encourage your sales team to invite you with them, but promise them you won't interfere. The sales professional is the CEO of a sales call. Visibility is crucial in today's overly technical approach to trying to reach customers and demonstrate a genuine concern for the customer.

Whose turn is it to tell the emperor he's naked?

Question any key executive working for you who doesn't personally object to at least one of your decisions per year. No top performer is that content, and no manager is that right all the time.

You're good, but not perfect. Meet with each of your senior staff, assuring them that all comments will be kept in confidence and you desire to learn from this experience. What can you do to help them? What do you do that drives them crazy? What policies stink? Which are outdated? What stifles creativity or the ability to sell more? They'll tell you the answers if the spirit of the meeting is upbeat and if you are approachable. If you don't hear anything negative, you may be too intimidating. Time to take a personal day and figure out what you can do to become approachable.

Of course, I'll buy 150 more boxes.

Feel guilty not buying cookies from the Girl Scout at your front door? Read Influence: The Psychology of Persuasion, *by Robert B. Cialdini, Ph.D.*

This book, written more than 17 years ago, is a perennial top-seller and a must-read for any manager. The book explores and dissects why and how humans process influencing behavior in all personal, social, and business settings. You will be amazed to learn just how simple and intimidating it is to influence people for good and bad. Read it before you read this Sunday's paper. Buy copies for your sales and management team, customer service, and marketing department, and make the book required reading. Discuss it at your next meeting—in the hallway, of course. And pass out the cookies you bought from a great salesperson you couldn't say no to: the Girl Scout.

What were those words to live by?

Be able to recite your personal and professional philosophy.

Every successful person you have ever met has a set of standards he or she abides by. Call it a philosophy, laws of living, success principles, rules—whatever the label, it is a deep, strong thread woven into the fabric of his or her character. You remember these people as long as you live. If they have been your mentor, they challenged you, encouraged you, stretched your mind, held you accountable, and let you sweat. They gave you room to risk, to live, to excel. Make sure your own philosophy is apparent in your persona; it is this energy and value system that attracts the top businesspeople to you and your organization. A great book to read on this subject is *The 7 Habits of Highly Effective People,* by Stephen Covey. His analysis of morals, ethics, energy management, and personal development is easy to read but packed with a wealth of material that will motivate you to change for the better. Don't leave home without it—a living philosophy, that is.

Volunteerism

Live your philosophy of business by helping others.

People judge a book by the cover at first, but it is actually the first three pages that determine whether the book gets read. Volunteerism is a tremendous way to show gratitude and give back to the community. It refreshes the soul and refuels our faith in mankind's willingness to help his neighbor. It is a noble effort and is rewarding without receiving monetary or material gifts.

Volunteerism is also a simple way to reach out in the community to attract like-minded individuals. Those who volunteer are well respected in the community. They get their pictures in the newspaper, newsletters, annual reports, and promotional pieces. Would you like these people on your team? Would they want you, a caring volunteer, as their leader? You bet. Fund-raisers, car washes, paint-a-thons, lake cleanup projects, cookie sales, pancake breakfasts, parade judging, sign painting, reading to the blind, church ushers—all contribute to our sanity and demonstrate our willingness to help. Even if we have intentions beyond the purely altruistic, the fact is we are helping those in need. And face it: People will also judge you by your actions outside of the work environment.

What will life be like after business?

Planning is great, but the thrill of business is all about the moment.

The clichés are endless with reference to living in the moment, the most famous one being, "I never heard anybody on their deathbed saying they wished they'd spent more time at the office." We have a good friend, a CEO who, at age 50, is starting to plan for a reduced work schedule by taking one extra week of vacation every year. He believes this approach will lessen the stress and increase his enjoyment of retirement or a less-than-40-hour workweek.

All too often, executives push themselves and their businesses to the limit in their work life. If they decide to call it quits, get fired, or lose a political battle, the transition to less than 100 mph is extremely stressful and psychologically challenging. Peter Drucker, the now-deceased author and total quality management guru, talked of the need to begin to plan the second half of your life before you get there. Begin to find hobbies and activities, worthy opportunities to volunteer, or a new business venture now. It gives you time to reflect and ease the strain of having to quit and go into a strange new world—a world of not working 60 hours a week.

In the meantime, enjoy the thrill of industry and business right now. Celebrate the big deal now. Rejoice in having attained the promotion now, instead of immediately looking at the next rung of your endless ladder that may be leaning against the wrong wall. Smile on your success and imagine how you'll feel looking back on this time knowing you did your best.

Controlling growth—
in more ways than one.

*Consistency in business practices and personal health
are vital to healthy organizations.*

Patience is a virtue that all motivated business professionals would love to have, but most really embrace the "get it now" philosophy. We want to make it happen now, close the deal now, grow the territory now, pay off debt now, hire more people now. And fast growth is good. To a point. Growth without adequate preparation, without advance notice to your "soon to be overwhelmed" staff, without analyzing the business from all angles, can be disastrous, to say the least.

The number-one goal of any corporation is to make a profit, but that doesn't mean a business has to grow in sales volume to generate a profit. Controlled growth, securing solid, profitable business (remember Pareto's 80/20 rule) is superior to keeping the machines humming with low profit margin business that chokes machine time. Are you growing methodically, in a reasonable state of chaos? Do you have an advisory board—formal or informal—to debate these issues?

And what about your physical growth? Yes, you. How's your health throughout all this? Is your waistline growing faster than the company's bottom line? Are you focused on maintaining your personal fitness to ensure you'll be around to cash in or cash out? Will you be able to do the things you've talked about doing in retirement or during the downshift phase of your career with your current fitness regimen? If not, now is the time to rethink priorities and set examples. Promoting fitness and health within your company while being an unfit specimen sends mixed signals to employees, shareholders, and family members. (Have you noticed? You rarely see an overweight CEO of a Fortune 500 organization. There's a reason for this.)

Self-analysis time

How are you doing with all this stuff?

Managing people is one of the most rewarding opportunities for individuals during their careers. Managing people is difficult, too. It's hard work. And in today's media-focused, litigious-happy marketplace, the pressure to do the right thing is tremendous. The challenges of sorting out people's personal issues, business aspirations, social issues, and expectations of corporate profits are hard to balance. Time and energy are two valuable commodities to any manager. All too often, your personal time and energy suffer because of job pressures. Finding a happy medium to balance life's tugs of family, fitness, work, financial obligations, and dreams warrants decisions to be made that don't always please everybody. Are you giving enough time for your own growth? Are you keeping your business skills sharp and updated? Are you being fair and honest with your expectations of what work gives you or, better yet, what you expect from your employees? Have you taken a vacation with your family recently? Did you have fun?

Did you call in to the office? Did you have the courage to leave your PDA on your dresser?

Succeeding in business is quite simple if we clearly define the basics of how to service the customer and how to treat others, but emotions tip us upside-down, making it tough to do the right thing. Be willing to risk being the first one to try something in your organization. If you're good at what you do, it'll work out fine. Even if it doesn't work, you'll have a better idea of what will work next time. Pick a few ideas a month to work on that seem to strike a chord in you. Promise yourself that you will do something different this week to make yourself better, smarter, happier, challenged, richer, more valuable. Write your résumé of your future self—your own ticket to succeed in any pursuit you feel compelled and passionate enough to undertake.

Disappear for a day

Take a full day every two months to do nothing but think, brainstorm, ponder, and plan.

When do you find time to think? When do you really sit and do nothing but contemplate the decisions ahead of you regarding new products, new services, growing or consolidating the business? Who will be your replacement or next executive vice president? When do you read with purpose, or sit with a pad of paper and outline your next six years in business or your family plans? The reality is that few CEOs, when interviewed on these topics, admit they are guilty of not stopping to think. They react, using intuition and gut. They utilize others' input and allow stereotypes and bias to guide their decisions without really analyzing the potential of other approaches. Fortunately, most CEOs are pretty bright, and their instincts and fast processing of information allow for better-than-average decision making. Yet imagine how much better the decisions or ideas could be with more thinking time.

Executives we've interviewed over the years all confide that they wish they had more time to stop, think, process, and dream. Why don't they, then? The number-one reason: They don't schedule the time.

Pick a day, block it out, have your assistant clear your schedule, and disappear to a beach, a park, a garden, a forest, a porch, a sailboat, you name it. No cell phones or PDAs. Just paper, pen, and cash for simple, light meals. Watch and feel what happens.

Section VI

Tips for Attracting/Retaining/Motivating
Top Sales Professionals

Visit the mine so you don't get the shaft.

Keep mobile employees in touch with corporate planning and direction. The independence of sales personnel is critical, but it can breed detachment.

Our mobile workforce has created an entirely different way leaders interface, evaluate, and motivate workers. Home-based managers, support crews, customer service, engineers, technicians, and salespeople need interaction with the boss. They are the real gold of the business—the lifeline and profit link to attracting new customers. They need assurance, feedback, and someone to bounce personal and business issues off of. Without this interaction, they can become distracted, isolated, and frustrated in their jobs. Spending a day with them, dining with them, visiting their family, giving them a forum to air their thoughts and get your advice, is the best use of your time as a manager. Find a way to meet with them a few times each quarter to maintain continuity and steady performance as well as to diagnose any problems.

The bottom line is: How much will I earn?

Commission plans must be understandable without a scientific calculator. Simplify them to show your sales reps how wealthy they can become.

A sales professional should be able to estimate—in the customer's parking lot, on a piece of paper—what his or her commission will be if he or she makes that particular sale. Simplifying commission plans is the first step to educating sales professionals to use their time for bigger sales and not waste time on futile deals. Salespeople are motivated by money, as well as by the need to persuade. If you give them fuel to fire up both these emotions, they will perform far better than they themselves ever expected.

High goals, high pay, high company earnings

*Create an incentive plan to allow salespersons
to earn more than 50 percent of their salary when
they attain some doable but tough numbers.
And don't lower the base salary, either.*

Want to find out if a new product is going to
make it in the market? Give the sales team
big commission dollars to sell it, and watch
what happens. FedEx Kinko's told us that waiting five
days for a package was foolish, but we didn't think about
it until it mentioned it. If there's a market, motivated
sales professionals will uncover the need better than any
marketing or focus group can. The extra commissions
you pay out will more than recoup any losses you had
in research that told you "maybe it'll sell, maybe not."

It's 11:00 P.M. Do you know where your customers are?

All salespeople and sales managers should have with them at all times the home phone numbers of the main contacts of their top 10 accounts.

In our years of recruiting sales and management talent, we've found the majority of these professionals can't put their hands on this critical data without a lot of digging. The 80/20 rule that says 80 percent of your business comes from 20 percent of your customers still hasn't hit home with them. The ability to connect with your top customers at a moment's notice for business or personal banter is the difference between a "long-term" and a "not anymore" customer. If your people don't have the information handy, they're probably not working with them enough.

Is it "broke" or doesn't it "work"?

Without the right skills and attitude, a technical degree doesn't guarantee the ability to manage a technical product or service division. The degree means the person who earned it can understand the process, not necessarily the prospect.

What about the person whose GPA was 1.8 out of 4.0 and still graduated as an engineer major? Yikes! Some of the sharpest, technically strong managers we have met were liberal arts and psychology majors. If the product features can be taught, don't hold out for an engineer to sell the product. There aren't that many engineers who like to sell in the first place, and sales personalities, in general, hold a high level of curiosity that shores up any technical deficiencies they may have. Many of the companies our firm has worked with avoid hiring sales individuals with engineering degrees because they're afraid the person will spend too much time on technical issues and too little time on selling and prospecting for new customers.

Short-term means long-term and long-term means short-term.

All sales personnel in your organization should have an attainable incentive plan from day one. If they don't, then don't refer to them as sales professionals.

Fact: The average sales professional stays with a company for three years. Fact: The average employee of a privately owned company in all work disciplines stays with a company 3.9 years. Convincing a salesperson to put out effort with the promise of a big payoff is crazy. True hunters are driven by the rewards. From day one, your salesperson has to see a carrot and trust that it won't disappear when he or she reaches it. As companies continue to merge, spin off, right size, supersize, you name it, sales professionals will not become top performers without a big-bang potential. The future is now. Long-term incentives don't hold the interest of sales professionals, and skepticism will keep promises of the future in the bottom drawer. The sooner you reward, the sooner the goals will be achieved. The shorter the time it takes to make the payoff goals, the longer the employee will stay with you and sell, sell, sell. Consider all these facts when designing sales training programs, recruiting strategies, incentive plans, and investment plans. How can you reward your salespeople today?

Section VII

Tips on Hiring
Top Sales Professionals

Hiring sales professionals is one of the toughest challenges for executives. Trying to calculate what personalities will fit into a company culture as well as the customer culture is a guessing game, but a manager can secure details when interviewing prospective sales candidates. Take good notes.

This section is devoted specifically to issues surrounding hiring sales professionals. You'll learn specific ways you can increase your odds of hiring great sales talent if you follow the tactics and formulas as outlined.

Raiders of the rival's ark

Snatching sales and management talent may look easier than it seems: the alternative

The number-one challenge facing business leaders today: securing and retaining human capital. As a CEO or key executive, you've probably heard or even spoken these words: "We have a better product, service, and benefits than our rivals. Let's lure the superstars to our firm…we need a person who knows our business…someone who can 'hit the street running'…a person with a 'book of business' that will ensure revenue…we just don't have the time to train someone without knowledge of our business." Sound familiar? Raiding the rival's ark to recruit top talent, promising them a richer compensation plan, fun workplace, promotions, benefits—even an equity stake—seems logical and lucrative enough. So why is it so difficult to raid the rival's ark of talent and bring them aboard yours?

Several issues face leaders today in need of human capital: Record high employment rates (95.5 percent), demographic shifts in an aging workforce, and reduction in potential workers are key issues. Evidence of a skeptical workforce, still uncertain about our economy, war, terrorism, etc., continues to impact decisions of candidates, who are treading cautiously when considering new employment. These factors affect the overall working population, but what about sales and management talent? What additional factors create psychological and business practice challenges when recruiting from the rival's ark?

Here's a list of key factors facing companies desirous to recruit top talent from rivals.

1. Hide 'n' seek for top talent. Mobile workers and technology thwart efforts to find talent quickly.
2. Non-compete agreements. The best will have an agreement and be bound or at least intimidated to remain to avoid any legal issues.
3. Counteroffer tactics work—just long enough to deflect defectors from leaving.
4. Emotional ties, fear of change, bonus money due, concerns with customer credibility, traitor labels, and guilt weigh heavily.
5. Top talent is most difficult to extract and satisfy— marginal performers will always look to leverage their position with a rival.

6. Reference checking is near impossible to secure accurate insights into character and skill sets. Marginal performers are able to hide in the fog of confidentiality, thus avoiding revealed weaknesses from vendor references.

7. Second-guessing by the raiders: "If they're so good, why did they let the top talent get away? What's wrong with this picture?"

8. Client relationships and "book of business" do not follow salespeople like lemmings to the sea. Studies show less than 15 percent of business survives the journey in the first 12–18 months.

9. Sometimes it works. A superstar jumps off the ark and swims to yours with no problem; the exception to the typical.

10. It's expensive. Compensation plans must entice superstars, and issues arise in the rank-and-file wanting equal pay.

11. Conflict arises as customers, torn between two vendors, could seek neutral vendors to avoid conflict and legal troubles; both arks lose.

Now what?

Having explored the challenges to raiding the rival's ark, here's a list of things you and your organization can do right now to offset the challenges and risks of raiding the rival's ark, while putting proactive systems in place to draw from a larger ocean of top talent around your ark. By designing and implementing efficient systems to improve the effectiveness of new sales and management professionals, you can avoid the wars on securing rival talent and attract those who want to board your ark or enter your markets.

1. Proactive hiring practices are mandatory. Don't wait till someone quits or is stolen to start a search. Plan B stands for "If it ain't broke, keep spare parts on hand in case."

2. Create specific initiatives and goals that this job must fulfill that are measurable and critical. Now require candidates to document they have achieved similar results in the past. This allows the measuring of consistent patterns of behavior and success.

3. Create written job descriptions, including core competencies and personality traits required for each sales and management position.

4. Install an incentive program that is performance-based.

5. Use a validated psychometric instrument to benchmark existing employees, and use it with each viable applicant. Gut intuition is strengthened with measurement.

6. Explore other industries that have successfully recruited talent from outside their industry.

7. Design or purchase a thorough, consistent, easy-to-implement sales training/product training program for every new employee. Raise the odds of success. Monitor progress carefully.

8. Consider retraining or realigning existing people on your ark. Are the workers on the ark in the right job for their skill sets?

9. Consensus hiring is out. Hiring managers must be accountable for their direct reports. Input from group interviews: yes. Final selection by consensus: NO.

10. Reward activity that leads to accomplishment. Create incentives that encourage and pay incentives for proactive behaviors that will lead to sales. This approach also provides management with feedback on process, learning, habits, intellect, drive, motivation, etc. (It's also insurance for jump-starting sales if the person fails and a newcomer picks up the trail.)

11. Interview approach: three interviews minimum, different interviewers, field trip, one interview during a public meal, references, phone interview to check energy and articulation, written case study, and a strategic plan for the first 120 days to be written by the applicant.

12. Applying these analytics and systems to evaluate and train top talent from the surrounding industries, you widen the talent pool, invite new ideas, increase the odds of top performers staying longer, and reduce costly turnover on your ark.

About the Authors

Ginni Garner is the owner and managing director of Sanford Rose Associates®—Cleveland East. She has more than a decade of experience in the executive search industry helping clients fill critical executive and management openings in service, technology, manufacturing, and healthcare organizations. Her career has spanned from small boutique firms to the publicly traded Heidrick & Struggles. Ginni's knowledge of corporate cultures, global business practices, and evolving client needs enables her to quickly assess and recruit compatible talent.

In addition to her practice serving global service organizations, she is a partner with the Healthcare Services Practice of Sanford Rose Associates. The practice focuses on recruiting executives for health systems, healthcare technology, and healthcare service organizations. She routinely completes senior leadership searches for C-level, SVP/GM, and VP roles as well as for key functional positions such as operations, sales, business development, technologies and human resources. Both emerging, privately held organizations as well as Fortune 1000 companies seek Ginni's expertise in executing assignments requiring proven talent and results-oriented experience.

In 2006 and 2007, Ginni was elected the president of the Sanford Rose Associates® Owners Association. She is a Certified Personnel Consultant (CPC) and M.B.A. She is an active member in the Northeastern Human Resources Planning Society (NOHRPS), Healthcare Financial Management Association (HFMA), and Direct Marketing Association (DMA). Ginni lives in Cleveland, Ohio, with her husband, Craig.

To reach Ginni directly: 440-893-9408or gkgarner@ sanfordrose.com.

Timothy J. Tolan is the owner and managing director of Sanford Rose Associates®—Charleston. SRA—Charleston has a primary focus on placing executive-level talent in the healthcare services, healthcare IT, insurance, and revenue cycle industries. Tim is a member of SRA's "President's Club" and is consistently recognized for operating one of the top-producing offices worldwide for SRA. He has conducted searches for CEOs, presidents, senior vice presidents, vice presidents of business development, product development and sales. He has worked with large-and small-cap companies as well as privately held and early-stage companies.

In addition to his executive search experience, Tim has been in the healthcare technology field for more than 25 years in executive-level positions for companies both public and private. His vast network of contacts comes from senior-level positions he held with ProxyMed, Inc., Healtheon/WebMD, ePhysician, and CITATION Computer Systems. Tim also spent 12 years in leadership roles in the hospital and provider marketplace. His broad healthcare experience allows him to focus on recruiting senior-level executives for a variety of healthcare clients, including healthcare delivery networks, diagnostics, outsourcing, and healthcare information technology companies.

Tim is a member of Healthcare Information Management Systems Society (HIMSS) and Healthcare Financial Management Association (HFMA). During his career, he has conducted personal development and training workshops for a variety of healthcare organizations. He is a graduate of the College of Healthcare Information Management Executives (CHIME).

Tim is a partner with the Healthcare Services Practice of Sanford Rose Associates. He also serves on the Board of Directors of the International Retained Search Association (IRSA). Tim has two children, enjoys public speaking, is an avid golfer, and loves to travel. Tim and his wife, Sue, reside on the coast of South Carolina. Tim can be reached directly at 843-579-3077 or at tjtolan@sanfordrose.com.

Photo: Danielle Riendeau

Dr. Russ Riendeau: nationally known keynote speaker and author of five books, his live presentations (www.HiringJam.com) combine live musical performance, humor, and audience interaction, delivering compelling messages on the art of talent acquisition, retention strategies, and resilience to business audiences and leaders of all kinds. Russ' programs have been called "the antidote to PowerPoint presentations" and support brain science research that shows learning retention and recall are enhanced when combined with music and humor. Russ was also the co-host of *The Business Doctor*, on Air America radio, in Chicago.

Since 1985, Russ has interviewed more business professionals than Oprah, Letterman, and Larry King combined—more than 75,000 business professionals in his career. He is senior partner and founder of The East Wing Search Group in Barrington, Illinois, an executive search firm servicing clients throughout North America.

Dr. Riendeau holds a Ph.D. in developmental psychology from Capella University and an M.A.

in applied behavioral sciences and a B.A. in psychology from National-Louis University. He's a member of Vistage International—the world's largest CEO membership organization, American Psychological Association, IRSA (International Retained Search Association), and the Civil Air Patrol. He's also a runner, cyclist, pilot, hockey player, and guitarist. Russ lives with his family in Barrington, Illinois. He can be reached at 847-391-0977, www.EastWingSearchGroup.com, or www.HiringJam.com.